Christmas with
the Holy Fathers

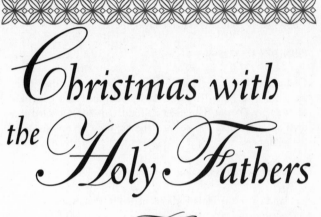

Christmas with the Holy Fathers

Compiled by Peter Celano

FOREWORD BY THOMAS HOWARD

PARACLETE PRESS
BREWSTER, MASSACHUSETTS

Christmas with the Holy Fathers

2008 First Printing

Copyright © 2008 by Paraclete Press, Inc.

ISBN: 978-1-55725-603-4

Quotations from the Holy Scriptures, as used by the editor, are from The New Jerusalem Bible, published and copyright © 1985 by Darton, Longman & Todd Ltd. and Doubleday, a division of Random House Inc., and are used by permission of the publishers.

Library of Congress Cataloging-in-Publication Data

Christmas with the Holy Fathers / edited by Peter Celano.
    p. cm.
  Includes bibliographical references.
  ISBN 978-1-55725-603-4
  1. Christmas--Prayers and devotions. 2. Catholic Church--Prayers and devotions. I. Celano, Peter.
  BV45.C587 2008
  242'.33--dc22
                                    2008028212

10 9 8 7 6 5 4 3 2 1

Published by Paraclete Press
Brewster, Massachusetts
www.paracletepress.com

Printed in the United States of America

CONTENTS

 FOREWORD

$\mathscr{T}$HE YEARLY RETURN OF ADVENT OFFERS to us a sequence of days in which we may turn our thoughts to a particularly rich series of events touching on the drama of our Redemption. Each event discloses a mystery, since in each case we find that what is played out on the stage of our own history reaches through the scrim that veils eternity from time, and presents to us mortals, in effect, the Love of God at work.

The whole season bids us reflect on the "coming" of God's Love to us in the person of His only begotten Son, Jesus Christ our Lord. The divine preparation for this great event is marked during the first few days of Advent with the Feast of the Immaculate Conception. And from there we move, with our Lady as it were, on to Christmas Eve with the shepherds, bringing with them the adoration of us all to the Incarnate One, and thence to the Morning of the Nativity itself. Christmas Night asks us to reflect on the call to holiness; and then we come upon St. Stephen's Day, which draws to our attention the first instance of our mortal flesh being asked to enter, via martyrdom, into the mystery of suffering that had been prepared, in God's counsels, for the newborn Infant from before the Creation. We mark with a Solemnity the mystery that crowns the young Virgin as Mother of God, with all that this means of God's munificence in drawing our lowly humanity into the highest precincts of His own action. And finally the Magi arrive to adore, bringing with them, as it were, the whole Gentile world for whom the gospel is to be opened.

In this small book we are invited to order our minds to the joyful task of meditating on these mysteries under the tutelage of the Bishops of Rome—a vastly encouraging invitation, as it happens, since it confirms for us, the faithful, the Lord's promise in choosing Peter to be the first of the long apostolic succession of servants of the servants of God who will be our shepherds until He returns in glory.

—Thomas Howard

 INTRODUCTION

*T*HERE IS NO BETTER TIME THAN ADVENT
and Christmas to turn our heads and hearts around to
the true meaning of our lives in Christ. Each year, we
anticipate his coming, and then we learn anew how to
best live into the meaning of Christ with us.

Still, there is probably no time of the year when
it is more difficult to focus on our Lord than right
about now. Slow changes have occurred over the last
generation or two, diminishing the season of Advent
for those of us who are old enough to remember earlier
times. No sooner do the decorations for Christmas go
up after (sometimes even before!) Thanksgiving, then
we begin to lose focus on the waiting and anticipation
that are meant to fill this season.

Customs have changed along the way. Caroling,
for instance, has faded away from what used to be
a delightful tradition in tightly knit neighborhoods.
And of course gift giving has become something that
our grandparents would never have imagined. Most
of our children spend more time dreaming about what
sorts of presents they will open on Christmas morning

than they do imagining what happened on that first night two millennia ago.

Christmas with the Holy Fathers offers an opportunity to you and your family to slow down and listen.

There's nothing more beautiful than the Christmas season as it is celebrated at St. Peter's Basilica and throughout Vatican City. If you are Catholic, you may well have watched on television, or perhaps even been there in person at some time in the past, as one of the Holy Fathers celebrated the Eucharist on Christmas Eve or Christmas morning. You may have actually heard some of the homilies, Angelus messages, and prayers that are excerpted in this book on the occasions when they were first given.

Many of these messages were originally delivered at difficult times in the history of the world. The Holy Father is a world leader, in addition to being the spiritual leader for more than one billion people. We have looked to the Holy Fathers for guidance in times of war and conflict, and often these Advent and Christmas messages have brought comfort and perspective to the people of the world, people of all faiths, in times of extraordinary need.

The lights, music, and liturgy of Advent, Christmas, and Epiphany continue for more than a month. The sermons given by the Holy Fathers throughout the ages at this time of year are among the most inspiring Christian literature ever delivered to an audience. Each Holy Father delivers special messages to the faithful on the great occasions of Advent, Christmas Eve, Christmas Day, the Solemnity of Mary the Mother of God, and on the Feast of the Epiphany. Their addresses were originally delivered orally and to great crowds.

At times, the pope speaks primarily in his capacity as the bishop of Rome, his oldest ecclesiastical title, and we have an opportunity to see how the Archdiocese of Rome relates to its spiritual father. But on each of these occasions, the pope speaks to all of us as a spiritual father. For Roman Catholics, the pope is "Papa," our true spiritual father, and we turn to him for guidance. We are rarely more attuned to hear the words of our spiritual fathers than on these special days leading to the birth of our Lord.

The personalities of the popes are varied and different. Each has his own way of communicating, and each, his unique messages for the essential life of the Church in that day. The following collection includes messages from Holy Fathers going back in history as far as Pope St. Leo the Great (AD 440–61). Pope Benedict XVI recently referred to Pope Leo as one of the most important popes in history. At one of his weekly Wednesday audiences, Pope Benedict said that Pope Leo "was one of the greatest incumbents of the See of Rome, the authority and prestige of which he strengthened. He is also the earliest pope whose sermons have come down to us, sermons he would address to the people who gathered around him during celebrations."[1]

And then, of course, we have included selections from the messages of Pope Benedict XVI, as well as from Pope John Paul II (1978–2005). In his very first message from the loggia of St. Peter's Basilica as pope, Benedict XVI referred to his predecessor as "the great Pope John Paul II" and since that time, Christians all over the world have been calling him Pope John Paul the Great, waiting for the day to come soon when we might add saint to his name.

Other favorite popes in history would include the following, many of whom are to be found in the following pages:

- Pope Saint Gregory I the Great (590–604)
- Pope Nicholas II (1059–61)
- Pope Saint Gregory VII (1073–85)
- Pope Innocent III (1198–1216)
- Pope Julius II (1503–12)
- Pope Paul III (1534–49)
- Pope Blessed Pius IX (1846–78)
- Pope Leo XIII (1878–1903)
- Pope Blessed John XXIII (1958–63)

The Christmas season has always been a special time for the Holy Fathers. Pope Saint Julius I, for example, was the one to mark December 25 as the official celebration of the great feast, in AD 350. December 25 is precisely nine months after March 25, the Feast of the Annunciation. (Ancient Christians also counted March 25 as the day of the crucifixion of Christ.) Pope Pius IX was the one to proclaim the dogma of the Immaculate Conception in 1854, to be celebrated on December 8, and then Pope Pius X remembered the occasion fifty years later (both excerpted below).

You likely have other Holy Fathers on your own list of favorites. We have included excerpts from as many of their messages as we could.

All of their messages are vital messages for the people of God. It is during this time of year, more than any other, that people of the other Christian denominations and other faiths turn to the voice of the Holy Father. He speaks to the world and the world listens to what he has to say. The words that follow, from the homilies of the popes during this most important of seasons, have drawn two millennia of people, from all parts of the world, to the holy Catholic Church.

ONE

Advent

INCLUDING THE FEAST OF
THE IMMACULATE CONCEPTION,
DECEMBER 8

*T*HE NAME *ADVENT* comes from the Latin word *advenire* (to come to), and refers to the coming of Jesus Christ to earth. This is the time of year during which the people of God begin preparing for the celebration of the Feast of Christmas that is to come, the annual birth of our Savior who comes into our midst.

The mystery of the Advent season is captured in remembering the original coming of Christ, as well as the Second Coming that we await in the future. The Messiah, the chosen one, will arrive in humble circumstances, foretold by the prophets. As Gabriel said to Mary, "Do not be afraid; you have won God's favour. Look! You are to conceive in your womb and bear a son, and you must name him Jesus. He will be great and will be called Son of the Most High. The Lord God will give him the throne of his ancestor David; he will rule over the House of Jacob for ever and his reign will have no end." (Luke 1:30–33)

He lives among us; he is *Emmanuel*, God with us. And that babe from the manger will come again in bodily form, and his kingdom shall have no end.

According to the customs of the ancient Church, the observance of Advent once included fasting for a period of forty days, just as we do during Lent, today. But during the Middle Ages, Advent was changed to a four-week period. The first Sunday of Advent is always the Sunday closest to November 30, the Feast of St. Andrew, and the fourth Sunday of Advent is always the Sunday before December 25.

In the pages that follow, you will be able to join the Holy Fathers in the great expectation and then celebration of the birth of the Messiah. Then ponder, explore, and celebrate with the Church of ages past, as we strive to make the birth of Christ real and present in our lives, today.

ADVENT
This Is a Time Distinct from All Others

POPE ST. LEO I
(AD 390–461)
Letter to the Bishops of Sicily

*T*HE RESTORATION OF MANKIND has indeed ever remained immutably fore-ordained in God's eternal counsel: but the series of events which had to be accomplished in time through Jesus Christ our Lord was begun at the Incarnation of the Word. Hence there is one time when, at the angel's announcement, the blessed Virgin Mary believed she was to be with child through the Holy Ghost and conceived: another, when without loss of her virgin purity the Boy was born and shown to the shepherds by the exulting joy of the heavenly attendants: another, when the Babe was circumcised: another, when the victim required by the Law is offered for him: another, when the three wise men attracted by the brightness of the new star arrive at Bethlehem from the East and worship the Infant with the mystic offering of Gifts.

This Is a Time of Preparation

POPE JOHN PAUL II
(1920–2005)

December 18, 2002

 ADVENT . . . HELPS US TO UNDERSTAND fully the value and meaning of the mystery of Christmas. It is not just about commemorating the historical event, which occurred some 2,000 years ago in a little village of Judea. Instead, it is necessary to understand that the whole of our life must be an "advent," a vigilant awaiting of the final coming of Christ. To predispose our mind to welcome the Lord who, as we say in the Creed, one day will come to judge the living and the dead, we must learn to recognize him as present in the events of daily life. Therefore, Advent is, so to speak, an intense training that directs us decisively toward him who already came, who will come, and who comes continuously.

Reflection on the Meaning of the Incarnation

POPE ST. LEO I
Letter to Flavian

$\mathcal{N}$OT ONLY IS GOD BELIEVED TO BE BOTH Almighty and the Father, but the Son is shown to be co-eternal with Him, differing in nothing from the Father because He is God from God, Almighty from Almighty, and being born from the Eternal one is co-eternal with Him; not later in point of time, not lower in power, not unlike in glory, not divided in essence: but at the same time the only begotten of the eternal Father was born eternal of the Holy Spirit and the Virgin Mary. And this nativity which took place in time took nothing from, and added nothing to that divine and eternal birth, but expended itself wholly on the restoration of man who had been deceived: in order that he might both vanquish death and overthrow by his strength, the Devil who possessed the power of death. For we should not now be able to overcome the author of sin and death unless He took our nature on Him and made it His own, whom neither sin could pollute nor death retain.

The Feast of Christ the King

POPE PIUS XI
(1857–1939)

December 11, 1925

*I*T HAS LONG BEEN A COMMON CUSTOM to give to Christ the metaphorical title of "King," because of the high degree of perfection whereby he excels all creatures. So he is said to reign "in the hearts of men," both by reason of the keenness of his intellect and the extent of his knowledge, and also because he is very truth, and it is from him that truth must be obediently received by all mankind. He reigns, too, in the wills of men, for in him the human will was perfectly and entirely obedient to the Holy Will of God, and further by his grace and inspiration he so subjects our free-will as to incite us to the most noble endeavors. He is King of hearts, too, by reason of his "charity which exceedeth all knowledge." And his mercy and kindness which draw all men to him, for never has it been known, nor will it ever be, that man be loved so much and so universally as Jesus Christ. But if we ponder this matter more deeply, we cannot but see that the title and the power of King belongs to Christ as man in the strict and proper sense too. For it is only as man that he may be said to have received from the Father "power and glory and a kingdom," since the Word of God, as consubstantial with the Father, has all things in common with him, and therefore has necessarily supreme and absolute dominion over all things created.

Christ Reveals Man to Himself

POPE JOHN PAUL II
Angelus
December 15, 1996

CHRIST IS THE LIGHT BECAUSE, in His divine identity, He reveals the Father's face. But He is so too because, being a man like us and in solidarity with us in everything except sin, He reveals man to himself. Unfortunately sin has obscured our capacity to know and follow the light of truth, and indeed, as the apostle Paul realized, it has exchanged "the truth about God for a lie" (Romans 1:25). By the Incarnation, the Word of God came to bring full light to man. In this regard the Second Vatican Council says that it is "only in the mystery of the Word made flesh that the mystery of man truly becomes clear" (*Gaudium et Spes*, No. 22).

Tenderly We Approach the Lord

POPE JOHN XXIII
(1881–1963)

December 23, 1959

WITH SUCH A WISH AND WITH SUCH A PRAYER, behold we have arrived, all of us, like Mary and Joseph, like the humble shepherds from the hills around Bethlehem, and like the Wise Men from the East, before the crib of our Newborn Savior. O Jesus, how tenderly we approach the simple crib! How sweet and devout are our hearts and feelings! How eager is our desire to unite all our labors in the great work of universal peace in Thy presence, Divine Author and Prince of Peace!

At Bethlehem all men must find their place. In the first rank should be Catholics. Today especially the Church wishes to see them pledged to an effort to make His message of peace a part of themselves. And the message is an invitation to check the direction of every act by the dictates of divine law, which demands the unflinching adherence of all, even to the point of sacrifice. Along with such a deepened understanding must go action. It is utterly intolerable for Catholics to restrict themselves to the position of mere observers. They should feel clothed, as it were, with a mandate from on high.

The effort, no doubt, is long and arduous. But Christmas means to all the certainty that nothing of men's good will is lost in whatever they perform in good will, perhaps without being entirely aware of it, for the coming of God's kingdom on earth and in order that the city of man may be modeled after the city of God. Ah, the city—the "city of God"—which St. Augustine hailed as resplendent with the truth that saves, with the charity that gives life and with the eternity that reassures!

He Inspires Us Toward Peace

—⟨⟩ POPE PIUS XI ⟨⟩—

December 23, 1922

*M*ANKIND IS IN NEED OF SPIRITUAL PEACE. We do not need a peace that will consist merely in acts of external or formal courtesy, but a peace which will penetrate the souls of men and which will unite, heal, and reopen their hearts to that mutual affection which is born of brotherly love. The peace of Christ is the only peace answering this description: "let the peace of Christ rejoice in your hearts" (Colossians 3:15). Nor is there any other peace possible than that which Christ gave to His disciples (John 14:27) for since He is God, He "beholdeth the heart" (1 Kings 16:7) and in our hearts His kingdom is set up. Again, Jesus Christ is perfectly justified when He calls this peace of soul His own for He was the first Who said to men, "all you are brethren" (Matthew 23:8). He gave likewise to us, sealing it with His own life's blood, the law of brotherly love, of mutual forbearance—"This is my commandment, that you love one another, as I have loved you" (John 15:12). "Bear ye one another's burdens; and so you shall fulfill the law of Christ" (Galatians 6:2).

From this it follows, as an immediate consequence, that the peace of Christ can only be a peace of justice according to the words of the prophet "the work of justice shall be peace" (Isaiah 32:17) for he is God "who judgest justice" (Psalms 9:5). But peace does not consist merely in a hard inflexible justice. It must be made acceptable and easy by being compounded almost equally of charity and a sincere desire for reconciliation. Such peace was acquired for us and the whole world by Jesus Christ, a peace which the Apostle in a most expressive manner incarnates in the very person of Christ Himself when he addresses Him, "He is our peace," for it was He Who satisfied completely divine justice by his death on the cross, destroying thus in His own flesh all enmities toward others and making peace and reconciliation with God possible for mankind (Ephesians 2:14).

Therefore, the Apostle beholds in the work of Redemption, which is a work of justice at one and the same time, a divine work of reconciliation and of love. "God indeed was in Christ, reconciling the world to himself" (2 Corinthians 5:19). "God so loved the world, as to give his only begotten Son" (John 3:16).

The Gift of Peace

POPE PIUS XI
December 20, 1929

*W*HEN THE HEAVENS were serene and earth was silent and night lay on the world, in secret, far from the crowd of men, the Eternal Word of the Father, having assumed the nature of man, appeared to mortals, and the heavenly regions echoed the heavenly hymn, "Glory to God in the highest and on earth peace to men of good will." This praise of Christian peace—the Peace of Christ in the Kingdom of Christ—setting forth the supreme desire of Our apostolic heart to which all our aims and our labors are directed, nearly touches the minds of Christians who withdrawn from the tumult and the vanities of the world in deep and hidden solitude have pondered on the truth of faith and the example of Him who brought peace to the world and left it as a heritage: "My peace I give to you."

This peace, truly so called, We wish for you from our heart, Venerable Brethren . . . as the sweet festival of the Nativity of Our Lord Jesus Christ approaches, which may be called the mystery of peace approaches, we with fervent prayer supplicate for that gift for him who is hailed as the Prince of Peace.

Imagine Most Holy Mary in Nazareth

POPE PAUL VI
(1897–1978)

Reflections at Nazareth
January 5, 1964

AT NAZARETH OUR VERY FIRST THOUGHTS must be turned toward Mary Most Holy, to offer her the tribute of our devotion and to nourish that devotion with reflections that will make it genuine, profound, and unique, in conformity with the plan of God. It is Mary who is full of grace, who is the Immaculate, the ever-virgin, the Mother of Christ, and hence God's Mother and ours, she who was assumed into heaven, our most blessed Queen, the model for the Church and our hope.

Before all else we offer our humble filial promise to venerate her with that special devotion which recognizes the wonders God has accomplished in her; with singular homage manifesting the most holy, pure affectionate, personal, and confident movements of our heart; with such devotion as causes her encouraging example of human perfection to shine upon the world from on high.

Then we present to her our requests for what is closest to our heart, because we wish to honor both her goodness and the power of her love and intercession. We pray that she may preserve in our hearts a sincere devotion to her. We beg her to give us understanding, desire, and then the peace of possessing purity of body and soul, purity in thought and word, art and love; the purity that the world of today attempts to shock and violate; the purity to which Christ has linked one of His promises, one of His beatitudes, that of penetrating into the vision of God Himself.

We ask therefore the favor of joining Our Lady, mother of the home at Nazareth, and her humble but courageous husband, St. Joseph, in their intimacy with Jesus Christ, her human and divine Son.

Nazareth—School of the Gospel

—⟡ POPE PAUL VI ⟡—
Reflections at Nazareth
January 5, 1964

*N*AZARETH IS THE SCHOOL IN WHICH we begin to understand the life of Jesus. It is the school of the Gospel. Here we learn to observe, to listen, to meditate, and to penetrate the profound and mysterious meaning of that simple, humble, and lovely manifestation of the Son of God. And perhaps we learn almost imperceptibly to imitate Him. Here we learn the method by which we can come to understand Christ. Here we discover the need to observe the milieu of His sojourn among us—places, periods of time, customs, languages, religious practices, all of which Jesus used to reveal Himself to the world. Here everything speaks to us; everything has meaning. Everything possesses twofold significance.

POPE JOHN PAUL II
Angelus
December 19, 1999

*T*ODAY'S SUNDAY BRINGS US to the last week of Advent: next Saturday is Christmas, and before the solemn midnight Mass, the Holy Door will be opened. . . .

The lights on the streets remind us of one aspect of this Feast, the most external, which although not negative in itself, nevertheless risks turning us away from the true spirit of Christmas. If, indeed, with good reason Christmas has become the feast of gifts, it is because it celebrates the gift par excellence that God has made to humanity in the person of Jesus. Thus, this must be lived in harmony with the meaning of the event, in a simple and sober manner.

In a very special way this year the Church invites us to prepare for this solemnity with joyful spiritual determination: with prayer, with a profound examination of conscience that leads to the sacrament of Reconciliation, with acts of charity toward one's neighbor, especially toward needy brothers and sisters.

This Sunday's Gospel presents the Virgin Mary in the act of welcoming the announcement of the Messiah's birth. For every Christian and every person of good will her attitude is a model of preparation for Christmas. . . . It is the attitude of faith, which consists of listening to the Word of God to give one's consent to it with the full acquiescence of mind and heart.

Christ's Mother teaches us to recognize the time of God, the favorable moment in which He touches our lives and asks for prompt and generous response. The mystery of the Holy Night, which historically happened two thousand years ago, must be lived as a spiritual event in the "today" of the Liturgy. The Word who found a dwelling in Mary's womb comes to knock on the heart of every person with singular intensity this Christmas.

By opening the Holy Door, the Church symbolically expresses that God has opened in front of all the way to salvation. It is up to each to respond, like Mary, with a personal and sincere yes and, in turn, open the space of his own existence to the love of God.

At Christmas, "the true light comes into the world, the one that enlightens every man (John 1:9); and

. . . May the example and intercession of Most Holy Mary help us to welcome the Savior, in order to receive fully the authentic gift of his Birth.

THE FEAST OF THE
IMMACULATE CONCEPTION
(December 8)

POPE PIUS IX
(1792–1878)

The Feast of the Immaculate Conception
December 8, 1854

GOD INEFFABLE—WHOSE WAYS ARE MERCY and truth, whose will is omnipotence itself, and whose wisdom "reaches from end to end mightily, and orders all things sweetly"—having foreseen from all eternity the lamentable wretchedness of the entire human race which would result from the sin of Adam, decreed, by a plan hidden from the centuries, to complete the first work of His goodness by a mystery yet more wondrously sublime through the Incarnation of the Word. This He decreed in order that man who, contrary to the plan of Divine Mercy had been led into sin by the cunning malice of Satan, should not perish; and in order that what had been lost in the first Adam would be gloriously restored in the Second Adam.

From the very beginning, and before time began, the eternal Father chose and prepared for his only-begotten Son, a Mother in whom the Son of God would become incarnate and from whom, in the blessed fullness of time, He would be born into this world. Above all creatures God so loved her that truly in her was the Father well-pleased with singular delight. Therefore, far above all the angels and all the saints so wondrously did God endow her with the abundance of all heavenly gifts poured from the treasury of His divinity that this mother, ever absolutely free of all stain of sin, all fair and perfect, would possess that fullness of holy innocence and sanctity that which, under God, one cannot even imagine anything greater, and which, outside of God, no mind can succeed in comprehending fully.

And indeed it was wholly fitting that so wonderful a mother should be ever resplendent with the glory of most sublime holiness and so completely free from all taint of original sin, that she would triumph utterly over the ancient serpent. To her did the Father will to give His only-begotten Son—the Son whom, equal to the Father and begotten by Him, the Father loves from His heart—and to give this Son in such a way that He would be the one and the same common Son of God the Father and of the Blessed Virgin Mary. It was she whom the Son Himself chose to make His

Mother and it was from her that the Holy Spirit willed and brought it about that He should be conceived and born from whom He Himself proceeds.

On the Fiftieth Anniversary

POPE PIUS X
(1835–1914)

February 2, 1904

*A*N INTERVAL OF A FEW MONTHS will again bring round that most happy day on which, fifty years ago, Our predecessor Pius IX, Pontiff of holy memory, surrounded by a noble crown of Cardinals and Bishops, pronounced and promulgated with the authority of the infallible Magisterium as a truth revealed by God that the Most Blessed Virgin Mary in the first instant of her conception was free from all stain of original sin. All the world knows the feelings with which the faithful of all the nations of the earth received this proclamation and the manifestations of public satisfaction and joy which greeted it, for truly there has not been in the memory of man any more universal or more harmonious expression of sentiment shown toward the august Mother of God or the Vicar of Jesus Christ.

And, Venerable Brethren, why should we not hope to-day after the lapse of half a century, when we renew the memory of the Immaculate Virgin, that an echo of that holy joy will be awakened in our minds, and that those magnificent scenes of a distant day, of faith and of love toward the august Mother of God, will be repeated? Of all this We are, indeed, rendered ardently desirous by the devotion, united with supreme gratitude for benefits received, which We have always cherished toward the Blessed Virgin; and We have a sure pledge of the fulfillment of Our desires in the fervor of all Catholics, ready and willing as they are to multiply their testimonies of love and reverence for the great Mother of God. But We must not omit to say that this desire of Ours is especially stimulated by a sort of secret instinct which leads Us to regard as not far distant the fulfillment of those great hopes to which, certainly not rashly, the solemn promulgation of the dogma of the Immaculate Conception opened the minds of Pius, Our predecessor, and of all the Bishops of the universe. . . .

[T]he first and chief reason, Venerable Brethren, why the fiftieth anniversary of the proclamation of the dogma of the Immaculate Conception should excite a singular fervor in the souls of Christians lies for us in that restoration of all things in Christ. . . . For can anyone fail to see that there is no surer or more direct road than by Mary for uniting all mankind in Christ and obtaining through Him the perfect adoption of sons, that we may be holy and immaculate in the sight of God? For if to Mary it was truly said: "Blessed art thou who hast believed because in thee shall be fulfilled the things that have been told thee by the Lord" (Luke 1:45); or in other words, that she would conceive and bring forth the Son of God, and if she did receive in her breast Him who is by nature Truth itself in order that "He, generated in a new order and with a new nativity, though invisible in Himself, might become visible in our flesh" (St. Leo the Great): the Son of God made man, being the "author and consummator of our faith"; it surely follows that His Mother most holy should be recognized as participating in the divine mysteries and as being in a manner the guardian of them, and that upon her as upon a foundation, the noblest after Christ, rises the edifice of the faith of all centuries.

Hail, Full of Grace, the Lord is with You!
(LUKE 1:28)

POPE JOHN PAUL II
December 8, 2004

WE ADDRESS THE VIRGIN MARY several times a day with these words of the archangel Gabriel. Let us repeat them with fervent joy today, on the Solemnity of the Immaculate Conception, remembering December 8, 1854, when Blessed Pius IX proclaimed this wonderful Dogma of the Catholic faith in this very same Vatican Basilica.

How great is the mystery of the Immaculate Conception that the Liturgy presents to us today! A mystery that never ceases to invite the contemplation of believers and inspires the reflection of theologians....

The Father chose her in Christ before the creation of the world, so that she might be holy and immaculate before him in love, preordaining her as the first fruits of filial adoption through the work of Jesus Christ (see Ephesians 1:4–5).

[T]he Immaculate Virgin, who marks "the very beginning of the Church, Bride of Christ, without spot or wrinkle, shining with beauty" (Preface), always precedes the People of God in the pilgrimage of faith, bound for the Kingdom of Heaven. In Mary's Immaculate Conception the Church sees projected and anticipated in her most noble member, the saving grace of Easter.

The Annunciation

POPE PIUS IX
December 8, 1854

WHEN THE FATHERS AND WRITERS of the Church meditated on the fact that the most Blessed Virgin was, in the name and by order of God himself, proclaimed full of grace by the angel Gabriel when he announced her most sublime dignity of Mother of God, they thought that this singular and solemn salutation, never heard before, showed that the Mother of God is the seat of all divine graces and is adorned with all gifts of the Holy Spirit. To them Mary is an almost infinite treasury, an inexhaustible abyss of these gifts, to such an extent that she was never subject to the curse and was, together with her Son, the only partaker of perpetual benediction. Hence she was worthy to hear Elizabeth, inspired by the Holy Spirit, exclaim: "Blessed are you among women, and blessed is the fruit of your womb."

A Prayer to the Blessed Virgin

POPE JOHN PAUL II
December 8, 2004

*T*O YOU, VIRGIN IMMACULATE, predestined by God above every other creature to be the advocate of grace and model of holiness for his people, today in a special way I renew the entrustment of the whole Church.

May you guide your children on their pilgrimage of faith, making them ever more obedient and faithful to the Word of God.

May you accompany every Christian on the path of conversion and holiness, in the fight against sin and in the search for true beauty that is always an impression and a reflection of divine beauty.

May you obtain peace and salvation for all the peoples. May the eternal Father, who desired you to be the immaculate Mother of the Redeemer, also renew in our time through you, the miracles of his merciful love. Amen!

Mary Our Mother

POPE PIUS X

February 2, 1904

*F*OR IS NOT MARY THE MOTHER OF CHRIST? Then she is our Mother also. And we must in truth hold that Christ, the Word made Flesh, is also the Savior of mankind. He had a physical body like that of any other man: and again as Savior of the human family, He had a spiritual and mystical body, the society, namely, of those who believe in Christ. "We are many, but one sole body in Christ" (Romans 12:5). Now the Blessed Virgin did not conceive the Eternal Son of God merely in order that He might be made man taking His human nature from her, but also in order that by means of the nature assumed from her He might be the Redeemer of men. For which reason the angel said to the shepherds: "To-day there is born to you a Savior who is Christ the Lord" (Luke 2:11). Wherefore in the same holy bosom of his most chaste Mother, Christ took to Himself flesh, and united to Himself the spiritual body formed by those who were to believe in Him. Hence Mary, carrying the Savior within her, may be said to have also carried all those whose life was contained in the life of the Savior.

Therefore all we who are united to Christ, and as the Apostle says are members of His body, of His flesh, and of His bones (see Ephesians 5:30), have issued from the womb of Mary like a body united to its head. Hence, though in a spiritual and mystical fashion, we are all children of Mary, and she is Mother of us all. Mother, spiritually indeed, but truly Mother of the members of Christ, who are we (St. Augustine).

The Devotion of the Rosary

POPE LEO XIII
(1810–1903)

September 1, 1883

*I*T HAS ALWAYS BEEN THE HABIT of Catholics in danger and in troublous times to fly for refuge to Mary, and to seek for peace in her maternal goodness; showing that the Catholic Church has always, and with justice, put all her hope and trust in the Mother of God. And truly the Immaculate Virgin, chosen to be the Mother of God and thereby associated with Him in the work of man's salvation, has a favor and power with her Son greater than any human or angelic creature has ever obtained, or ever can gain. And, as it is her greatest pleasure to grant her help and comfort to those who seek her, it cannot be doubted that she would deign, and even be anxious, to receive the aspirations of the universal Church.

This devotion, so great and so confident, to the august Queen of Heaven, has never shone forth with such brilliancy as when the militant Church of God has seemed to be endangered by the violence of heresy spread abroad, or by an intolerable moral corruption, or by the attacks of powerful enemies. Ancient and modern history and the more sacred annals of the Church bear witness to public and private supplications addressed to the Mother of God, to the help she has granted in return, and to the peace and tranquility which she had obtained from God. Hence her illustrious titles of helper, consoler, mighty in war, victorious, and peace-giver. And amongst these is specially to be commemorated that familiar title derived from the Rosary by which the signal benefits she has gained for the whole of Christendom have been solemnly perpetuated. There is none among you, Venerable Brethren, who will not remember how great trouble and grief God's Holy Church suffered from the Albigensian heretics, who sprung from the sect of the later Manicheans, and who filled the South of France and other portions of the Latin world with their pernicious errors, and carrying everywhere the terror of their arms, strove far and wide to rule by massacre and ruin. Our merciful God, as you know, raised up against these most direful enemies a most holy man, the illustrious parent and founder of the Dominican Order. Great in the integrity of his doctrine, in his example of virtue, and by his apostolic labors, he proceeded undauntedly to attack the enemies of the

Catholic Church, not by force of arms, but trusting wholly to that devotion which he was the first to institute under the name of the Holy Rosary, which was disseminated through the length and breadth of the earth by him and his pupils. Guided, in fact, by divine inspiration and grace, he foresaw that this devotion, like a most powerful warlike weapon, would be the means of putting the enemy to flight, and of confounding their audacity and mad impiety. Such was indeed its result.

Thanks to this new method of prayer—when adopted and properly carried out as instituted by the Holy Father St. Dominic—piety, faith, and union began to return, and the projects and devices of the heretics to fall to pieces. Many wanderers also returned to the way of salvation, and the wrath of the impious was restrained by the arms of those Catholics who had determined to repel their violence.

The Virgin Mary's Guidance

POPE PIUS IX
December 8, 1854

*L*ET ALL THE CHILDREN of the Catholic Church, who are so very dear to us, hear these words of ours. With a still more ardent zeal for piety, religion, and love, let them continue to venerate, invoke and pray to the most Blessed Virgin Mary, Mother of God, conceived without original sin. Let them fly with utter confidence to this most sweet Mother of mercy and grace in all dangers, difficulties, needs, doubts, and fears. Under her guidance, under her patronage, under her kindness and protection, nothing is to be feared; nothing is hopeless. Because, while bearing toward us a truly motherly affection and having in her care the work of our salvation, she is solicitous about the whole human race. And since she has been appointed by God to be the Queen of Heaven and earth, and is exalted above all the choirs of angels and saints, and even stands at the right hand of her only-begotten Son, Jesus Christ our Lord, she presents our petitions in a most efficacious manner. What she asks, she obtains. Her pleas can never be unheard.

TWO

Christmas Eve

THE IMPORTANCE OF
CHRISTMAS EVE

*T*HIS IS THE DAY when the Christmas season officially begins, following the weeks of Advent that have led up to it. As we inherited from Jewish worship, Christmas begins on the evening before the day. The account of Creation in Genesis reads that "an evening and a morning were the first day."

For many Christians, the Mass or Christmas Vigil that happens on Christmas Eve afternoon or evening is one of the liturgical highlights of the year. It used to be that these great services would begin late in the evening and then culminate at midnight with a celebration of the birth of our Lord. In some parts of the world, such as the Philippines or certain places in Latin and South America, these beautiful worship services may last for several hours, and then continue with a feast of foods and gifts into the early hours of Christmas morning.

Christmas originated as a compound word for "Christ Mass." This is a time of profound and meaningful celebration. Sir Walter Scott once wrote,

"On Christmas Eve, the bells were rung / On Christmas Eve, the mass was sung."

"Today is born our Savior"
(RESPONSORIAL PSALM)

POPE JOHN PAUL II
Midnight Mass
December 24, 2000

ON THIS NIGHT, THE ANCIENT yet ever new proclamation of the Lord's birth rings out. It rings out for those keeping watch, like the shepherds in Bethlehem two thousand years ago; it rings out for those who have responded to Advent's call and who, waiting watchfully, are ready to welcome the joyful tidings which in the liturgy become our song: *Today is born our Savior.*

The Christian people keep watch; the entire world keeps watch on this Christmas night which is linked to that unforgettable night a year ago, when the Holy Door of the Great Jubilee was opened, the Door of grace opened wide for all.

The Darkness of the World

POPE BENEDICT XVI
(1927-   )

December 24, 2007

THE MESSAGE OF CHRISTMAS makes us recognize the darkness of a closed world, and thereby no doubt illustrates a reality that we see daily. Yet it also tells us that God does not allow Himself to be shut out. He finds a space, even if it means entering through the stable; there are people who see His light and pass it on. Through the word of the Gospel, the angel also speaks to us, and in the sacred liturgy the light of the Redeemer enters our lives. Whether we are shepherds or "wise men" the light and its message call us to set out, to leave the narrow circle of our desires and interests, to go out to meet the Lord and worship Him. We worship Him by opening the world to truth, to good, to Christ, to the service of those who are marginalized and in whom He awaits us.

A Feast of Light

POPE JOHN PAUL II
December 24, 2001

THE PEOPLE WHO WALKED IN DARKNESS have seen a great light. (Isaiah 9:2)

Every year we listen again to these words of the prophet Isaiah in the moving context of the liturgical re-evocation of Christ's Birth. Every year these words take on new meaning and cause us to relive the atmosphere of expectation and hope, of amazement and joy typical of Christmas.

To the people, oppressed and suffering, who walked in darkness, there appeared "a great light." A truly "great" light indeed, because the light which radiates from the humility of the crib is the light of the new creation. If the first creation began with light (see Genesis 1:3), how much more splendid and "great" is the light which inaugurates the new creation: it is God Himself made man!

Christmas is an event of light, it is the feast of light: in the Child of Bethlehem the primordial light once more shines in humanity's heaven and dissipates the clouds of sin. The radiance of God's definitive triumph appears on the horizon of history in order to offer a new future of hope to a pilgrim people.

The Child Is Born for Everyone

POPE JOHN PAUL II
December 24, 2001

THE GRACE OF GOD HAS APPEARED, offering salvation to all. (Titus 2:11)

Our hearts this Christmas are anxious and distressed because of the continuation in various parts of the world of war, social tensions, and the painful hardships in which so many people find themselves. We are all seeking an answer that will reassure us.

The passage from the Letter to Titus which we have just heard reminds us that the birth of the Only-begotten Son of the Father has been revealed as "an offer of salvation" in every corner of the earth, at every time in history. The Child who is named "Wonder-Counselor, God-Hero, Father-Forever, Prince of Peace" (Isaiah 9:6) is born for every man and woman. He brings with him the answer which can calm our fears and reinvigorate our hope.

A Prayer to Mary Our Mother

POPE JOHN XXIII

*H*OLY IMMACULATE MARY, help all who are in trouble. Give courage to the faint-hearted, console the sad, heal the infirm, pray for the people, intercede for the clergy, have a special care for nuns; may all feel, all enjoy your kind and powerful assistance, all who now and always render and will render you honor, and will offer you their petitions. Hear all our prayers, O Mother, and grant them all. We are all your children: Grant the prayers of your children. Amen forever.

"In the Depths of the Night a Voice Resounds"
(POLISH CHRISTMAS CAROL)

~~ POPE JOHN PAUL II ~~
December 24, 1996

*I*N THE FIRST READING, the prophet Isaiah says: "The people who walked in darkness have seen a great light; on those who dwelt in a land of deep darkness, on them has light shined" (Isaiah 9:2). The light shone because "to us a child is born, to us a son is given" (9:6).

The same Christmas carol identifies that voice in the night: "Come, shepherds, God is born for you; hasten to Bethlehem to greet the Lord." It is the same voice which resounds in the passage of the Gospel of Luke just proclaimed: "In that region there were shepherds out in the fields keeping watch over their flock by night. And an angel of the Lord appeared to them, and the glory of the Lord shone around them, and they were filled with fear. The angel said to them, 'Be not afraid; for behold I bring you good news of a great joy which will come to all the people. For to you is born this day in the city of David a Saviour, who is Christ the Lord. And this will be a sign for you: you will find a babe wrapped in swaddling cloths and lying in a manger' " (Luke 2:8–12). The Christmas carol continues: "[The shepherds] set off, and in the manger they found the Child with all the signs which had foretold his birth. They adored him as God."

We Are Witnesses to the Love of Christ

POPE JOHN PAUL II
Midnight Mass
December 24, 2000

THE WORD CRIES IN A MANGER. His name is Jesus, which means "God saves," because "he will save his people from their sins" (Matthew 1:21).

It is not a palace which sees the birth of the Redeemer, destined to establish the eternal and universal Kingdom. He is born in a stable and, coming among us, he kindles in the world the fire of God's love (see Luke 12:49). This fire will not be quenched ever again.

May this fire burn in our hearts as a flame of charity in action, showing itself in openness to and support of our many brothers and sisters sorely tried by want and suffering!

Lord Jesus, whom we contemplate in the poverty of Bethlehem, make us witnesses to Your love, that love which led You to strip Yourself of divine glory, in order to be born among us and die for us.

The Message of Christmas for All Nations and People

POPE PIUS XII
(1876–1958)

Christmas Message, 1942

$\mathcal{M}$Y DEAR CHILDREN OF THE WHOLE WORLD:

As the Holy Christmas Season comes round each year, the message of Jesus, Who is light in the midst of darkness, echoes once more from the crib of Bethlehem in the ears of Christians and re-echoes in their hearts with an ever new freshness of joy and piety. It is a message which lights up with heavenly truth a world that is plunged in darkness by fatal errors. It infuses exuberant and trustful joy into mankind, torn by the anxiety of deep, bitter sorrow. It proclaims liberty to the sons of Adam, shackled with the chains of sin and guilt. It promises mercy, love, peace to the countless hosts of those in suffering and tribulation who see their happiness shattered and their efforts broken in the tempestuous strife and hate of our stormy days.

The church bells, which announce this message in every continent, not only recall the gift which God made to mankind at the dawn of the Christian Era; they also announce and proclaim a consoling reality of the present, a reality which is eternally young, living and life-giving; it is the reality of the "True Light which enlighteneth every man that cometh into this World," and which knows no setting. The Eternal Word, Who is the Way, the Truth, and the Life, began His mission of saving and redeeming the human race by being born in the squalor of a stable and by thus ennobling and hallowing poverty.

He thus proclaimed and consecrated a message which is still, today, the Word of Eternal Life.

THREE

The Feast of the Nativity of Our Lord

CHRISTMAS MORNING
Come to the Humble Cradle

POPE PIUS XII

Christmas Message, 1944

THE HUMBLE, MEAN CRADLE OF BETHLEHEM, by its wonderful charm, focuses the attention of all believers. Deep into the hearts of those in darkness, affliction, and depression there sinks and pervades a great flood of light and joy.

Heads that were bowed lift again serenely, for Christmas is the feast of human dignity, "the wonderful exchange by which the Creator of the human race, taking a living body, deigned to be born of a virgin, and by His coming bestowed on us His divinity" (first antiphon of first vesper for the feast of the Circumcision).

But our gaze turns quickly from the Babe of the Crib to the world around us, and the sorrowful sigh of John the Evangelist comes to our lips: "and the light shines in darkness, and the darkness did not comprehend it" (John 1:5).

Good News of Great Joy

~~ POPE BENEDICT XVI ~~
December 25, 2005

I BRING YOU GOOD NEWS OF A GREAT JOY ...
for to you is born this day in the city of David a Savior, who is Christ the Lord. (Luke 2:10–11)

Last night we heard once more the angel's message to the shepherds, and we experienced anew the atmosphere of that holy night, Bethlehem Night, when the Son of God became man, was born in a lowly stable and dwelt among us. On this solemn day, the angel's proclamation rings out once again, inviting us, the men and women of the third millennium, to welcome the Savior. May the people of today's world not hesitate to let him enter their homes, their cities, their nations, everywhere on earth!

In the millennium just past, and especially in the last centuries, immense progress was made in the areas of technology and science. Today we can dispose of vast material resources. But the men and women in our technological age risk becoming victims of their own intellectual and technical achievements, ending up in spiritual barrenness and emptiness of heart. That is why it is so important for us to open our minds and hearts to the Birth of Christ, this event of salvation which can give new hope to the life of each human being.

"Wake up, O man! For your sake God became man" (St. Augustine). Wake up, O men and women of the third millennium! At Christmas, the Almighty becomes a child and asks for our help and protection. His way of showing that He is God challenges our way of being human. By knocking at our door, He challenges us and our freedom; He calls us to examine how we understand and live our lives.

The modern age is often seen as an awakening of reason from its slumbers, humanity's enlightenment after an age of darkness. Yet without the light of Christ, the light of reason is not sufficient to enlighten humanity and the world. For this reason, the words of the Christmas Gospel: "the true Light that enlightens every man was coming into this world" (John 1:9) resound now more than ever as a proclamation of salvation. "It is only in the mystery of the Word made flesh that the mystery of humanity truly becomes clear" (*Gaudium et Spes*, No. 22). The Church does not tire of repeating this message of hope reaffirmed by the Second Vatican Council, which concluded forty years ago.

God Made Man

POPE BENEDICT XVI

December 25, 2005

AT CHRISTMAS WE CONTEMPLATE GOD made man, divine glory hidden beneath the poverty of a Child wrapped in swaddling clothes and laid in a manger; the Creator of the Universe reduced to the helplessness of an infant. Once we accept this paradox, we discover the Truth that sets us free and the Love that transforms our lives. On Bethlehem Night, the Redeemer becomes one of us, our companion along the precarious paths of history. Let us take the hand which he stretches out to us: it is a hand which seeks to take nothing from us, but only to give.

With the shepherds let us enter the stable of Bethlehem beneath the loving gaze of Mary, the silent witness of His miraculous birth. May she help us to experience the happiness of Christmas, may she teach us how to treasure in our hearts the mystery of God who for our sake became man; and may she help us to bear witness in our world to His truth, his love, and his peace.

He Has Come to Free Us All

POPE ST. LEO I
Sermon on the Feast of the Nativity

*O*UR SAVIOR, DEAR FRIENDS, was born today: let us rejoice! For there is no proper place for sadness, when we keep the birthday of the Life, which destroys the fear of mortality and brings to us the joy of promised eternity. No one is kept from sharing in this happiness. There is for all one common measure of joy, because as our Lord the destroyer of sin and death finds none free from charge, so is He come to free us all. Let the saint exult in that he draws near to victory. Let the sinner be glad in that he is invited to pardon. Let the gentile take courage in that he is called to life.

Cause for Rejoicing

POPE ST. LEO I
Sermon on the Feast of the Nativity

*L*ET US BE GLAD IN THE LORD, dearly-beloved, and rejoice with spiritual joy that there has dawned for us the day of ever-new redemption, of ancient preparation, of eternal bliss. For as the year rolls round, there recurs for us the commemoration of our salvation, which promised from the beginning, accomplished in the fullness of time will endure for ever; on which we are bound with hearts up-lifted to adore the divine mystery: so that what is the effect of God's great gift may be celebrated by the Church's great rejoicings.

Living Bread from Heaven

JESUS CHRIST SAID OF HIMSELF: I am the Living Bread descended from Heaven. Therefore, Bethlehem, the place where our Lord was born, has been called the House of Bread; for He who fed our hearts to satiety appeared there in the substance of flesh.

God Has Entered Human History

POPE JOHN PAUL II

December 25, 1999

THAT WHICH WAS FROM THE BEGINNING . . . which we have . . . touched with our hands, concerning the Word of life . . . we proclaim to you. (1 John 1:1–2)

On this solemn day on which we are commemorating the birth of the Lord Jesus Christ, we perceive the truth, the power and the joy of the apostle John's words.

Yes, in faith, our hands have touched the Word of Life; they have touched the One who, as we recited in the Canticle, is the image of the invisible God, the first-born of all creation. Through Him and in Him all things were created (see Colossians 1:15–16). This is the mystery of Christmas that we perceive with deep emotion. . . .

God entered human history and came to walk the paths of this earth, to enable everyone to become God's children.

We Partake in This Birth

Sermon on the Feast of the Nativity

*I*N CHRIST, BORN OF THE VIRGIN'S WOMB, the nature does not differ from ours, because His nativity is wonderful. For He Who is true God, is also true man, and there is no lie in either nature. "The Word became flesh" by exaltation of the flesh, not by failure of the Godhead: which so tempered its power and goodness as to exalt our nature by taking it, and not to lose His own by imparting it. In this nativity of Christ, according to the prophecy of David, "truth sprang out of the earth, and righteousness looked down from heaven." In this nativity also, Isaiah's saying is fulfilled, "let the earth produce and bring forth salvation, and let righteousness spring up together." For the earth of human flesh, which in the first transgressor, was cursed, in this Offspring of the Blessed Virgin only produced a seed that was blessed and free from the fault of its stock. And each one is a partaker of this spiritual origin in regeneration; and to every one when he is re-born, the water of baptism is like the Virgin's womb; for the same Holy Spirit fills the font, Who filled the Virgin, that the sin, which that sacred conception overthrew, may be taken away by this mystical washing.

POPE JOHN PAUL II
December 25, 1999

WE COULD SAY THAT THIS EVENING'S RITE takes on a more familiar dimension. Indeed the diocesan family is setting out on its own jubilee journey, in special unity with the churches spread throughout the world. It has been preparing for this great event for a long time, first through the Synod and then with the City Mission. The devout participation of the city and of the whole diocese testifies that Rome is aware of the mission of universal concern and of exemplarity in faith and love which God's Providence has entrusted to it. Rome knows well that this service is rooted in the martyrdom of the apostles Peter and Paul and has always found new sustenance in the witness of the multitude of martyrs and saints who have marked the history of our Church.

Dear brothers and sisters, the Holy Year, which begins today, calls us too to continue on this road. It invites us to respond joyfully and generously to the call to holiness, to be increasingly a sign of hope in today's society. . . .

Happy Birthday

Sermon on the Feast of the Nativity

THE BIRTH OF CHRIST is the source of life for Christian people, and the birthday of the Head is the birthday of the body. Although every individual that is called has his own order, and all the sons of the Church are separated from one another by intervals of time, yet as the entire body of the faithful being born in the font of baptism is crucified with Christ in His passion, raised again in His resurrection, and placed at the Father's right hand in His ascension, so with Him are they born in this nativity.

The Church in the World

THE CHURCH HAS THE MISSION to announce to the world . . . the highest and most needed message that there can be: the dignity of man, the call to be sons of God. It is the powerful cry, which from the Manger of Bethlehem to the furthest confines of the earth resounds in the ears of men at a time when that dignity is tragically low.

The holy story of Christmas proclaims this inviolable dignity of man with a vigor and authority that cannot be gainsaid—an authority and vigor that infinitely transcends that which all possible declarations of the rights of man could achieve.

Christmas, the Great Feast of the Son of God Who appeared in human flesh, the feast in which heaven stoops down to earth with ineffable grace and benevolence, is also the day on which Christianity and mankind, before the crib, contemplating the "goodness and kindness of God our Savior" become more deeply conscious of the intimate unity that God has established between them.

The Birth of the Savior of the World, of the Restorer of human dignity in all its fullness, is the moment characterized by the alliance of all men of goodwill. There to the poor world, torn by discord, divided by selfishness, poisoned by hate, love will be restored, and it will be allowed to march forward in cordial harmony, toward the common goal, to find at last the cure for its wounds in the peace of Christ.

Light in Darkness

POPE PIUS XII
Christmas Message, 1942

HIS LIGHT CAN OVERCOME THE DARKNESS, the rays of His love can conquer the icy egoism which holds so many back from becoming great and conspicuous in their higher life. To you, crusader-volunteers of a distinguished new society, live up to the new call for moral and Christian rebirth, declare war on the darkness which comes from deserting God, of the coolness that comes from strife between brothers. It is a fight for the human race, which is gravely ill and must be healed in the name of conscience ennobled by Christianity.

The Lesson of Silence—A Prayer

POPE PAUL VI
Reflections at Nazareth
January 5, 1964

THE LESSON OF SILENCE: may there return to us an appreciation of this stupendous and indispensable spiritual condition, deafened as we are by so much tumult, so much noise, so many voices of our chaotic and frenzied modern life. O silence of Nazareth, teach us recollection, reflection, and eagerness to heed the good inspirations and words of true teachers; teach us the need and value of preparation, of study, of meditation, of interior life, of secret prayer seen by God alone.

A Prayer to the Child of Bethlehem

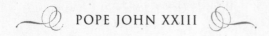 POPE JOHN XXIII

O sweet Child of Bethlehem,
grant that we may share with all our hearts
in this profound mystery of Christmas.
Put into the hearts of men and women this peace
for which they sometimes seek so desperately
and which you alone can give to them.
Help them to know one another better,
and to live as brothers and sisters,
children of the same Father.
Reveal to them also your beauty, holiness, and
  purity.
Awaken in their hearts
love and gratitude for your infinite goodness.
Join them all together in your love.
And give us your heavenly peace. Amen.

FOR DECEMBER 26
*Make Room for the Son of God
Who Is Given to Us at Christmas*

POPE JOHN PAUL II

Angelus

December 26, 1996

*T*HE JOY OF CHRISTMAS ALSO FILLS OUR HEARTS today, while the Evangelist's wonderful announcement continues to re-echo throughout the Church: "And the Word became flesh and dwelt among us" (John 1:14). The reason for our joy is precisely this: today Christ is born for us: he brings the world peace.

In the mystery of Christmas, the paschal mystery is already present. Jesus comes into the world to fulfill his mission of salvation which will culminate in his crucifixion and in the extraordinary event of his Resurrection. The martyrdom of St. Stephen, which we are commemorating today, brings us somehow to contemplate this reality leading us to the heart of our faith.

Filled with the Holy Spirit, the proto-martyr Stephen was stoned for confessing his adherence to the divine King, born in the stable of Bethlehem.

The Only Begotten One who comes into the world invites every believer to choose the path of life (see Deuteronomy 30:19). This is the profound meaning of His coming among us. Loving the Lord and obeying His voice, the deacon Stephen chose Christ, Life and Light for every man and woman. By choosing the truth, he became, at the same time, a victim of the mystery of iniquity present in the world.

As in times past and even in this century, the Church, in witnessing to the truth, finds herself experiencing the supreme trial of martyrdom in many of her children. She is aware that, in accepting the Son of God, she is called to share His destiny: as she lives the joy of His birth, united to Him, so she is also ready to follow Him in the supreme act of Paschal love.

In making room in our heart for the Son of God, who is given to us at Christmas, we also renew our will to follow Him faithfully on the way of the Cross, certain that our ultimate goal is the blissful encounter with the Father.

We pray to the Virgin Mary, Mother of God and Queen of martyrs, that she may guide us and sustain us on our journey to Christ whom we contemplate in the crib.

POPE PAUL VI
Reflections at Nazareth
January 5, 1964

WE CANNOT DEPART WITHOUT RECALLING briefly and fleetingly some fragments of the lesson of Nazareth. . . . Now we hear its echo reverberating in the souls of men of our century. It seems to tell us: blessed are we, if in poverty of spirit we learn to free ourselves from false confidence in material things and to place our chief desires in spiritual and religious goods, treating the poor with respect and love as brothers and living images of Christ.

Blessed are we, if, having acquired the meekness of the strong, we learn to renounce the deadly power of hate and vengeance, and have the wisdom to exalt above the fear of armed force the generosity of forgiveness, alliance in freedom and work, and conquest through goodness and peace.

Blessed are we, if we do not make egoism the guiding criterion of our life, nor pleasure its purpose, but learn rather to discover in sobriety our strength, in pain a source of redemption, in sacrifice the very summit of greatness.

Blessed are we, if we prefer to be the oppressed rather than the oppressors, and constantly hunger for the progress of justice.

Blessed are we, if for the Kingdom of God in time and beyond time we learn to pardon and to persevere, to work and to serve, to suffer, and to love.

We shall never be deceived.

In such accents do we seem to hear His voice today. Then, it was stronger, sweeter, and more awe-inspiring: it was divine. But as we try to recapture some echo of the Master's words, we seem to be won over as His disciples and to be genuinely filled with new wisdom and fresh courage.

FOUR

Solemnity of Mary, Mother of God

(JANUARY 1)

MARY, OUR MOTHER

ON THE EIGHTH DAY OF CHRISTMAS, the Catholic Church celebrates the Solemnity of Mary, Mother of God. Her motherhood was singular in history and cause for the salvation brought by her Son. In the life of Mary, her divine motherhood was a foretaste and foreshadowing of her glory to come.

This is a day on which Catholics and others may celebrate the unique role of Mary in the history of salvation. "Called in the Gospels 'the Mother of Jesus,' Mary is acclaimed by Elizabeth, at the prompting of the Spirit and even before the birth of her son, as 'the mother of my Lord.' In fact, the One whom she conceived as man by the Holy Spirit, who truly became her Son according to the flesh, was none other than the Father's eternal Son, the second person of the Holy Trinity. Hence the Church confesses that Mary is truly 'Mother of God'" (*Catechism of the Catholic Church*, 495).

Born of a Woman

POPE JOHN PAUL II
January 1, 2004

*W*HEN THE TIME HAD FULLY COME, *God sent forth his Son, born of woman.* (Galatians 4: 4)

Today, the liturgy of the Octave of Christmas presents to us the *icon of the Mother of God*, the Virgin Mary. The apostle Paul points her out as the "woman" through whom the Son of God entered the world. Mary of Nazareth is the *Theotokos*, the One who "gave birth to the King of Heaven and earth for ever" (Entrance Antiphon).

At the beginning of this new year, let us place ourselves with docility at the school of Mary. We want to learn from her, the Holy Mother, *how to accept in faith and prayer the salvation* that God never ceases to offer to all who trust in His merciful love.

Justice for All People

POPE JOHN PAUL II
January 1, 2004

*E*VERY YEAR IN THIS CHRISTMAS SEASON *we return in spirit to Bethlehem* to adore the Child lying in the manger. Unfortunately, in the land in which Jesus was born tragic conditions endure. In other parts of the world, hotbeds of violence and conflict are also still smoldering. However, we must persevere *without giving in to the temptation to despair.* All are asked to make an effort to see that the fundamental rights of the person are respected, by constantly teaching respect for the law. With this in mind, it is necessary to strive to transcend "the logic of simple *justice* and to be open also to the logic of *forgiveness.*" Indeed, "there is no peace without forgiveness!"

A Day for Peace

POPE JOHN PAUL II
January 1, 2000

*T*AKING INTO ACCOUNT THE START of a new year, today's liturgy expresses good wishes to all people of good will with these words: *"The Lord lift up his countenance upon you, and give you peace"* (Numbers 6:26).

May the Lord grant you peace! This is the Church's wish to all humanity on the first day of the new year, a day dedicated to the celebration of the World Day of Peace. . . . I am thinking at this moment of the prayer meeting for peace which gathered representatives of the world's main religions in Assisi, in October 1986. We were still in the period of the so-called Cold War: together, we prayed to avert the great threat of a conflict which seemed to menace humanity. In a certain sense, we gave voice to everyone's prayer, and God heard his children's supplication. Even if we had to note the outbreak of dangerous local and regional conflicts, we were nonetheless spared the great world conflict which had loomed on the horizon. This is why, with greater awareness, we wish one another peace as we cross the threshold of the new century: *may the Lord lift up his countenance upon you.*

FIVE

The Feast of the Epiphany

(JANUARY 6)

EPIPHANY COMES FROM THE GREEK word *Epiphania*, which means "to make known, or reveal." The celebration of Epiphany originated in the Eastern Church in the year AD 361, as the day to remember the birth of Christ. (Only the churches in Armenia still mark the Nativity as January 6, rather than December 25.)

Since the Middle Ages, Epiphany has marked three events in the early life of Jesus: the visit of the three Magi to the infant Jesus, Christ's baptism in the Jordan River (this is the primary event of the Epiphany in Orthodox churches), and Christ's first miracle at the wedding in Cana. All three of these events are central to the meaning of Epiphany.

A Necessary Sequel to Christmas

POPE ST. LEO I
Sermon on the Feast
of the Epiphany

AFTER CELEBRATING THE DAY on which immaculate virginity brought forth the Savior of mankind, the venerable feast of the Epiphany, dearly beloved, gives us continuance of joy, that the force of our exultation and the fervor of our faith may not grow cool, in the midst of neighboring and kindred mysteries. For it concerns all men's salvation, that the infancy of the Mediator between God and men was already manifested to the whole world, while He was still detained in the tiny town. For although He had chosen the Israelite nation, and one family out of that nation, from whom to assume the nature of all mankind, yet He was unwilling that the early days of His birth should be concealed within the narrow limits of His mother's home: but desired to be soon recognized by all, seeing that He deigned to be born for all. To three wise men, therefore, appeared a star of new splendor in the region of the East, which, being brighter and fairer than the other stars, might easily attract the eyes and minds of those that looked on it, so that at once that might be observed not to be meaningless, which had so unusual an appearance. He therefore who gave the sign, gave to the beholders understanding of it, and caused inquiry to be made about that, of which He had thus caused understanding, and after inquiry made, offered Himself to be found.

The Light of Christ

POPE JOHN PAUL II
January 6, 1999

THE LIGHT SHINES IN THE DARKNESS, and the darkness has not overcome it. (John 1:5)

Today the whole liturgy speaks of the light of Christ, of that light which was kindled on the Holy Night. The same light which led the shepherds to the stable in Bethlehem shows the way, on the day of Epiphany, to the Magi who have come from the East to worship the King of the Jews, and it shines brightly for all men and women and for all peoples who long to meet God.

In his spiritual quest, the human being already enjoys a guiding light: it is reason, through which he can find the way, although gropingly (see Acts 17:27), toward his Creator. But since it is easy to lose the way, God Himself has come to his aid with the light of Revelation, which attained its fullness in the Incarnation of the Word, the eternal Word of truth.

Epiphany celebrates the appearance in the world of this divine Light in which God has reached out to the faint light of human reason. Today's solemnity suggests the close relationship between faith and reason, the two wings on which the human spirit rises to the contemplation of truth. . . .

Be Like a Heavenly Light

POPE ST. LEO I
*Sermon on the Feast
of the Epiphany*

WHOEVER LIVES FAITHFULLY in the Church and "sets his mind on the things which are above, not on the things that are upon the earth," is in some ways like the heavenly light. And while he himself keeps the brightness of a holy life, he points out to many the way to the Lord like a star. In this regard, you ought to all help one another, so that in the kingdom of God, which is reached by right faith and good works, you may shine as the sons of light: through our Lord Jesus Christ, Who with God the Father and the Holy Spirit lives and reigns for ever and ever. Amen.

POPE ST. LEO I
Sermon on the Feast
of the Epiphany

$\mathscr{T}$AUGHT BY THESE MYSTERIES of divine grace, let's celebrate with joy the day of our first-fruits and the commencement of the nations' calling: "giving thanks to" the merciful God "who made us worthy," as the Apostle says, "to be partakers of the lot of the saints in light: who delivered us from the power of darkness and translated us into the kingdom of the Son of His love." Since, as Isaiah prophesied, "the people of the nations that sat in darkness, have seen a great light, and they that dwelt in the land of the shadow of death, upon them hath the light shined."

The Lord said, "nations that did not know thee, shall call on thee: and people that were ignorant of thee, shall run together unto thee." On this day "Abraham saw and was glad," when he understood that the sons of his faith would be blessed in his seed that is in Christ, and foresaw that by believing he should be the father of all nations.

It was this day that David sang of in the psalms: "all nations that thou hast made shall come and worship before Thee, O Lord: and they shall glorify Thy name." And again: "The Lord has made known His salvation: He has openly showed his righteousness in the sight of the nations." This in good truth we know to have taken place ever since the three wise men aroused in their far-off land were led by a star to recognize and worship the King of heaven and earth. And surely, their worship of Him exhorts us to imitation, so that, as far as we can, we should serve our gracious God who invites us all to Christ.

He Shows Us the Way to the Father

POPE JOHN PAUL II
January 6, 1999

𝒞HRIST IS NOT ONLY THE LIGHT that illumines man's way. He also became the path for his uncertain steps toward God, the source of life. One day he will say to the Apostles: "I am the way, and the truth, and the life; no one comes to the Father but by me. If you had known me, you would have known my Father also; henceforth you know him and have seen him" (John 14:6–7). And in response to Philip's objection, he will add: "He who has seen me has seen the Father . . . I am in the Father and the Father in me" (John 14:9–11). The epiphany of the Son is the epiphany of the Father.

Was this not the reason, after all, for Christ's coming into the world? He Himself declared that He had come to "make the Father known," to "explain" to people who God is, to reveal His face, His "name" (John 17:6). Eternal life consists in meeting the Father (see John 17:3).

AND SO OUR THOUGHTS LEAVE NAZARETH and range those mountains of Galilee which once provided the natural backdrop for the words of the Divine Teacher. We lack time and sufficient strength to proclaim at this moment the divine message intended for the entire universe. But we cannot neglect to glance at the nearby mount of the beatitudes, which are the synthesis and summit of evangelical preaching, and to listen to the echoes of that discourse which, in this mysterious atmosphere, now seem audible to us.

It is the voice of Christ promulgating the New Testament, the new law which both absorbs and surpasses the old, and raises human endeavor to the very peak of perfection. . . . Christ in His Gospel has spelled out for the world the supreme purpose and the noblest force for action and hence for liberty and progress: love. No goal can surpass it, be superior to it, or supplant it. The only sound law of life is His Gospel. The human person reaches his highest level in Christ's teaching. Human society finds therein its most genuine and powerful unifying force.

We believe, O Lord, in Thy word; we will try to follow and live it.

118

PERMISSIONS
AND ACKNOWLEDGMENTS

$\mathscr{S}$ELECTIONS FROM THE WRITINGS of the Holy Fathers that predate World War II are taken from a variety of sources. Most of the selections from the sermons of Pope John Paul II and Pope Benedict XVI, as well as other modern Holy Fathers, are taken from the Vatican's Web site, and all are used by permission. They are copyright © 2008 by Libreria Editrice Vaticana. The selections from Pope Paul VI's "Reflections at Nazareth" are taken from *The Pope Speaks*, Vol. 9, no. 3, 1964.

NOTES

1. Catholic News Service, "St. Leo the Great was one of the greatest popes in history, says Benedict XVI," March 5, 2008.

ABOUT PARACLETE PRESS

Who We Are

Paraclete Press is an ecumenical publisher of books and recordings on Christian spirituality. Our publishing represents a full expression of Christian belief and practice—from Catholic to Evangelical, from Protestant to Orthodox.

Paraclete Press is the publishing arm of the Community of Jesus, an ecumenical monastic community in the Benedictine tradition. As such, we are uniquely positioned in the marketplace without connection to a large corporation and with informal relationships to many branches and denominations of faith.

We like it best when people buy our books from booksellers, our partners in successfully reaching as wide an audience as possible.

What We Are Doing
Books

Paraclete Press publishes books that show the richness and depth of what it means to be Christian. Although Benedictine spirituality is at the heart of all that we do, we publish books that reflect the Christian experience across many cultures, time periods, and houses of worship.

We publish books that nourish the vibrant life of the church and its people—books about spiritual practice, formation, history, ideas, and customs.

We have several different series of books within Paraclete Press, including the best-selling Living Library series of modernized classic texts; A Voice from the Monastery—giving voice to men and women monastics about what it means to live a spiritual life today; award-winning literary faith fiction; and books that explore Judaism and Islam and discover how these faiths inform Christian thought and practice.

Recordings

From Gregorian chant to contemporary American choral works, our music recordings celebrate the richness of sacred choral music through the centuries. Paraclete is proud to distribute the recordings of the internationally acclaimed choir Gloriæ Dei Cantores, who have been praised for their "rapt and fathomless spiritual intensity" by *American Record Guide*, and the Gloriæ Dei Cantores Schola, which specializes in the study and performance of Gregorian chant. Paraclete is also the exclusive North American distributor of the recordings of the Monastic Choir of St. Peter's Abbey in Solesmes, France, long considered to be a leading authority on Gregorian chant performance.

YOU MAY ALSO BE INTERESTED IN...

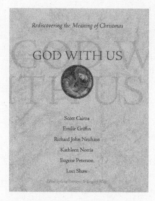

God With Us
*Rediscovering the
Meaning of Christmas*

Edited by Greg Pennoyer
and Gregory Wolfe

ISBN: 978-1-55725-541-9
$29.95, Hardcover

God With Us is a companion for those who want to experience Christmas as the early Christians once did, set in the larger context of Advent and Epiphany. Through daily meditations, Scripture, prayer, illuminating history and fine art, we experience what saints have glimpsed through the ages—the wonder of God made flesh.

Contributors:
Scott Cairns • Emilie Griffin • Richard John Neuhaus
Kathleen Norris • Eugene Peterson • Luci Shaw

Available from most booksellers or through Paraclete Press
www.paracletepress.com • 1-800-451-5006
Try your local bookstore first.